THE FIVE THINGS
YOU CAN'T F&CK UP IN YOUR BUSINESS

DAN DRISCOLL

ISBN: 978-1-6847-1806-1 (sc)
ISBN: 978-1-6847-1805-4 (e)

Library of Congress Control Number: 2020901559

Lulu Publishing Services rev. date: 01/24/2020

CONTENTS

Preface vii

Introduction ix

Chapter 1 Knowing Your Ideal Client 1

Chapter 2 Having the Right Offer 9

Chapter 3 Having the Right Pricing Strategy 21

**Chapter 4 Giving Your Employees a Long-Term
Reason to Show Up for Work** 35

Chapter 5 Having a Good Plan to Keep Your Clients 47

Conclusion 55

Appendix 59

PREFACE

I want to first thank you for picking up my book. It means a lot to me to know that you are taking time out of your day to learn how to improve the profitability of your current business or maybe even to start planning your next venture. I take your time seriously, and I wrote this book to be a quick read that if applied and executed properly could add a huge bottom line impact to your endeavor. I love to simplify things. I may also drop really good ideas in just a sentence or two, so don't be scared to stop and reread a line or two. I really write a lot differently than other authors.

But before we get into the book, I want to tell you a little bit about myself. I am a Florida cracker, born and raised. My family grew up in St. Petersburg, which is located on Florida's west coast. By the way, if you have not been, I suggest you visit. The beaches and people are amazing. Anyway, from an early age I always knew that I wanted to have my own business. I used to play with LEGO and built my empire as early as five years old. I read "Think and Grow Rich" the Napoleon Hill classic, before I was in middle school. I have, since birth, been obsessed with business.

My parents could tell my extreme enthusiasm for business and earning money at an early age. I was the kid who was always trying to sell something to turn a profit. The older I got, the more I realized that business was about a lot more than hustle. I also learned that hard work actually makes you less money in business over the long term. This took a while to learn, and I might still be learning it. Over the last twenty years, I have been a student of the game of business. I have owed several businesses, earned an MBA from a top business school (almost worthless, but I paid enough, so I need to mention it), and consulted with hundreds of businesses about how to increase their profitability. All in all, the lessons I learned did not come only from reading but through application and reading. These lessons came from rolling up my sleeves and noticing what aspects are essential to having a business. These lessons also did not come cheap. Every mistake I made was expensive.

The first business I started and grew was in the federal contracting area. I grew this business to over $11 million in sales with more than fifty employees. This experience was valuable because in this process, I realized my true mission, helping business owners win the game of business. I have noticed so many business owners are playing a game that can't be won. They put in long hours and make less and less money each year. These business owners have built themselves a prison, not the business they once envisioned.

My mission is to make the game winnable for business owners. To allow each business owner to truly have an enterprise that can stand alone, that can survive generations. One they can be proud of.

> All you need is the plan, the road map, and the courage
> to press on to your destination. (Earl Nightingale)

INTRODUCTION

There is only one boss. The customer. And he can
fire everybody in the company from the chairman on
down, simply by spending his money somewhere else.
—Sam Walton

So how complicated is it really to own and run a business? I mean, some of the most successful entrepreneurs started out of a garage with almost no business training. Many of them even made horrible operating mistakes when running their businesses and yet still thrived. Learning how to run a business from my study is not hard; it just takes time. Business mastery can be broken down into two parts. Part 1, the focus of this book, is on how to get the business started. Now when I say get the business started, I do not mean only the first few months of operation. I'm talking about the first seven to ten years of running the business. In my experience, 98 percent of the businesses I have worked with were still in their startup phases. Even as you move to the second part of owning a business, never forget the first part. I always think about spring training and practicing the basics. **Businesses succeed or fail for the simplest reasons**. For example, you could run a multimillion-dollar organization and only focus on the first part of running a business. Many do.

In my experience, when a business moves into the second part of business ownership, they often run into problems. The second phase is all about optimizing the business for profit and cash flow. Although both of these are important in the first part of running a business, they are much more focused on in the second part. Think about how everyone hates the bean counters. Well, the second part of the business is all about the bean counting. For instance, getting a board and a management team are highlights in the second part of running a business. As well as aligning organizational goals with profit metrics. **Just to let you know, expense reduction is the fastest way to add profit to a business.** Many business owners think that they can exercise off all the wasted expenses. But in business, this is simply not the case. You can't outsell waste and inefficacies; you have to remove them to truly optimize the business.

The reason I want to talk about the second part is to help you understand that so much information about running a business is based on the second part. This information, unfortunately, is not relevant for the majority of business owners. I'm sure you have read a book and thought, *That's great, but it's not for me.* Right? Again, that will not be this book. I'm going to give you the must knows, the essentials. This book is written by a real business owner for a real business owner.

Are you ready to get started? Sweet. Pay attention and get your mind ready to learn. Remember, in business and in life, the master focuses on practicing the essentials. Save the advanced topics for the Harvard grads. If you master these five principles—know your ideal client, know your offer, have the right pricing strategy, have a good plan to keep your employees, and have a really good plan to keep your clients—you will succeed in business. It is that simple.

I wrote this book to give you the information you need to either start a business or optimize your current business. I feel strongly that no matter how much business experience you have, you will find this information valuable. I have structured this book to be an easy read. I spent a lot of time thinking about what business information was fluff and what could be deleted. When I wrote my last two books, *The Four Paths to Success as a Federal Vendor* and *The Sales Burnout Survival Guide*, I realized that long books were not helping anyone. The real value in writing is to give the relevant information and delete the fluff. I know when I was in school, we always had this concept around fluffing up the report. This idea of creating fluff was burned into our brains. When we had writing assignments in school, we had per-character word requirements. Do you remember that? They were teaching us to fluff up things, a horrible idea in business, right? Yes. In life, this concept of fluff is a complete time waste. And it will kill your business. **In business, the first rule is keep it simple**

stupid, or KISS for short. If you want to hire and train an employee, for example, how important is it to simplify that process? Have you ever worked at a company where they trained you for three months on things that you would never use? It seemed the four or five things that you needed to know were buried in the manual, but they were not reinforced.

Almost every job at your company, from the janitor to the CEO, can be broken down into about five essential things. I know you may not follow me 100 percent yet, but you will. Just stay with me. Think about it right now. What are the five most important things each of your employees needs to do from your perspective? Now go ask the employees what five things they think are most important for them to do. I wonder if any of your five made their top five. This is why it's essential to practice the basics. If we all did the five most important things in running a business at a high level, the other things would take care of themselves. This same rule applies to your employees and in life. This is also the concept I used to delete the fluff when writing this book.

When you finish this book, you will have learned a lot about yourself, not just your business. It is important that you grow with your business. For example, you will learn how to simplify and delete unnecessary tasks from your daily routine. But more important, how to delete tasks and rules that do not matter for your employees. **As a business owner, time is money, and your job is to simplify and remove waste.**

This book will be effective not just for the words but for the actions you take after reading it, the application. I'm not a great writer by any means, so please don't obsess on my typos. To prove my point, on my last two books, I relied heavily on the readers of my first editions for edits. Thank you for that, by the way. **But the reason this book will be effective for you are the questions that I'm going to ask you.** This book will serve as a guide to get your business profitable and to improve how you interact with your business and employees. You will learn that how you interact with the business is actually the most important thing in the success of the business. **A successful business is simply a self-sustaining organization run and owned by its employees.** The employees may not get all the bottom-line profits, but they should get a share of the rewards. Employees should feel empowered to help grow the organization and its profitability. If your employees are just showing up every day, then you have a job, not a business.

The more you can wrap your head around this concept of employee ownership, the better you will be able to design an organization that is capable of surviving for generations. The business is the people who work at the business, not the owner of the business. **In my opinion, aligning compensation and employee awards around the profitability of the business is the only way to create a truly lasting business.** Jeff Bezos has from day 1 at Amazon made his employees owners by tying bonuses to company objectives and being generous with stock options to make sure all his employees think and act like owners. Think about it for a second. How many top people have left your organization over the years? How many top people have left Amazon? When you treat your people right, you can keep and recruit the best people. Another interesting fact is that the best hires often come from where? In my experience, they have come through referrals. And how do you get referrals? From employees who think like owners and truly care about the organization enough to refer their friends.

As you read this book, pretend that I'm sitting right next to you, coaching you through the exercises. Play full out as you read this book. Know the more effort you put into this book and the exercises, the better your results. Ninety-six percent of businesses never make it ten years. And out of the 4 percent that make it, how many do you think are profitable? Trust me, not many. I know you are likely thinking of a few unprofitable business owners you know. They are everywhere. Someone is always f*cking up his or her business. In all the consulting I have done with businesses over the last decade, I never found a business that had a ten-year plan. Do you think this may be part of the reason 96 percent don't make it ten years? I mean seriously, they barely had a one-year plan. **This brings up the first lesson: As a business owner, your vision is the ceiling for the business. If you want to succeed in business, you must have absolute certainty in its outcome. And you must have a vision so great it compels you and your team to play full out. Your vision is the single biggest thing you bring to the business.**

Since we all want to win, what does winning the game of business look like? I mean really winning? I have asked this question and thought about it a lot over the years. When I first thought about it, I came up with the idea that a business that won the game was profitable and paid the owner's personal overhead. Then I said, "Maybe it's when you have a big enough business to pay for all the toys you could ever want." As I kept progressing through the phases of business ownership, I realized more money did not make me feel victorious. I actually felt that the more money I made, the more stressed I was about the business. For example, I now had a bigger business with many more things to be worried about. And the bigger the business got, the more things could go wrong. I used to worry about the economy and my employees making catastrophic mistakes. Some of these stressors were even so petty in the grand scheme of things they should not have been on my radar. I mean, I worried about an employee making a $200 expense without asking me first. All this when our company did over $11 million in sales. That was .00002 percent of my revenue. Ridiculous, right? Do you think that was something I should have been focusing on? I started asking, "What bothers me about my business? How can I fix it? And if I fix it, would that make my business a winner?"

So I got to work on asking these questions. The first problem I uncovered was the economy. This is a huge problem, by the way. The media knows how to get everyone emotionally charged about the economy, providing day by day anxiety for many business owners. I asked, "How can I make sure that no matter what happens in the economy, my business will be okay?" As I asked this question, I started to think about how to protect my business and cash flow. I came up with the fact that I would need multiple noncorrelated income streams. I needed to add income streams that would do better as the economy slowed, for example. Think about this for a minute. **How could you diversify your business between customer types and product offerings, thereby reducing the risk any one customer stream has on the health of your organization?** For example, if you only dealt with carpet cleaning for homeowners, how much will they cut back in a recession? I imagine lower-income homeowners would possibly even stop cleaning the carpets. But if you also did commercial cleaning for hotels, do you think the hotels can afford to not clean the carpets during a recession? Yes, you are right. They can't stop cleaning; who would stay at a dirty hotel. Putting together a simple plan like this, which we will go over more in chapter 5, can seriously reduce the risk to your business caused by shifts in the economy.

The next problem I dealt with was the stress of my employees making mistakes. As a business owner, you have to provide an organization that allows your employees to grow or they will either leave or decompose, both providing very little true value to the enterprise. Unfortunately, no one grows without making mistakes. Do you remember how many mistakes you made when you first started the business? Mistakes are not bad; they are a necessary part of growth. The key is to have a way to tell if an employee is making an abnormal number of mistakes based on his or her tenure with your organization and to have a system to measure and hold your employees accountable for this standard.

Back to the need for growth for your employees. Have you ever heard the term "dead-end job"? Just to be clear, you do not want to have one of these at your organization. These dead-end jobs are also really not in demand right now. Anyway, we cover more of that in chapter 4. Employee growth only comes at the expense of the control of the owner. It relies on having a system in place to evaluate whether employees are making abnormal mistakes. Trust me, employees will make mistakes. That is normal. As a business owner, you have to be willing to allow your employees to grow so you can grow. If you, the business owner, do not grow in your business at some point, you will be stressed, miserable, or bored. If you fail to grow, you will have effectively given yourself one of those dead-end jobs that we are trying not to give our employees. I mean, do you feel like an employee of your business now? Do you think that is something that needs to change? Trust me you are not alone.

The challenge is how do you grow and at the same time not worry about your employees messing up. The answer is dashboards. How cool would it be to know if someone was making costly mistakes or just doing something differently than you would do it? Would it save you some stress to have a check engine light that went off if your business was in trouble? That is what a dashboard can do for your business. By the way, the dashboard can also tell you if you are winning the game of business. I mean, how could you play a game without a scoreboard? The dashboard is your scoreboard, and it tells you how you are doing. More important, it lets you know what plays you need to run. Managing a business without a scoreboard is like driving blindfolded; it's only a matter of time before you crash.

The reason these systems are so valuable is they give you the optics to not wonder if your business is doing well. Dashboards give you the ability to know the key drivers of your business success and the key vulnerabilities you need to watch. There are many ways to succeed in business. **As an owner, you need to be concerned with the outcome, not the path your team uses to get to the desired outcome**. For example, Suzie may not follow the same steps in opening mail you used for years. She may actually take fewer steps and get a better outcome when she handles the mail. But this can only happen if you have a system of controls that allows you to give her the ability to find the best way to perform the task. I know this may sound funny, but business owners often micromanage tasks pettier than this one. And more important, they micromanage the tasks that have no impact on the bottom line of the organization. When we talk about dashboards, we want you to have a check engine light that says Suzie did a great job or one that says Suzie needs some coaching. For opening the mail, the dashboard could be as simple as late payment charges on your organization's financial dashboard. If your late fees are going up on your statement, it likely means Suzie is not opening the mail fast enough and paying the bills quickly enough. Does that make sense? We have to have something to compare our employees output to other than gut feelings. Our gut will often guide us to make short term emotional decisions with our employees while dashboards will equip us with the tools to make long term financially beneficial decisions.

In short, to win the game of business, you have to have: (1) Clarity on which are the most important outcomes for the business to pursue (2) Correctly prioritize resources to those outcomes (3) a system to evaluate employee performance based on assigned outcomes, not tasks so you can give up some or all of the daily control to your employees, and (4) multiple flows of income so you are confident your business can weather any economic storm. Once you have these four items in place, can you see how you may start to walk and talk a little differently? As soon as you reach this level, how much different would owning your business be? Remember, the biggest limits on a business's growth are the limits the owner creates. Can the owner give up controls to the right people and have a system in place to make sure they are meeting the outcomes necessary? Can the owner relax and enjoy the business? Once the owner answers yes to these questions and has the right rules, controls, and dashboards in place, the business has the option to truly scale. Think about it. How big can your business grow now with you continue doing your current tasks? If you fail to give up any of these tasks, how long will your employees stay with you if they can't grow? If you think about it, do you really want to double the size of the business if it doubles the amount of work you have to do? Many business owners sabotage their growth plans because they refuse to remove key items from their plate that would allow growth, these owners refuse to give up the certainty. As a business owner, your goal should be to never run more than 80 percent capacity. Running at under capacity allows for a vacuum to form and new opportunities and growth to occur. As you begin working over this threshold, you need to find out what lower-value tasks you can delegate or eliminate from your role. If you are overworked and stressed there is a good chance your employees are overworked and stressed and this combination is not good for growing an organization.

As we go through these five simple things, you will learn how to create a more successful business setup. But more important, you will learn how to win the game of business. You will also see you don't need a fancy degree or a great CFO to succeed in business. **Success is about knowing what you need to do and then doing it consistently**. Think about Michael Jordan. How many jump shots did he shoot each day in practice? It was over a thousand! Do you think he needed a refresher on jump shots? Or do you think he realized this was the only way to master basketball? How often do you think you should come back to the basics in your business? How often are you going to practice? Business is not a set it and forget it endeavor. You must constantly come back and ask these same questions over and over with your team. In business, being proactive is the key to success. By reading this book and taking time to work on the business, you are practicing for the championship game. You are starting the journey to business mastery. Just as Michael Jordan practiced every day, you will also want to focus on the basics and train daily in your business.

Remember, very few people win in business. The winners in business were not necessarily the smartest, but they were the hardest workers who knew their outcomes. They committed to the basics. They asked for help and had a vision so large it compelled them to dig deep and work harder. They were not scared to hire people smarter than them. They did not think small. They knew their desired outcomes and what it would take to get there. Are you up for a challenge? Do you really have what it takes to succeed? Can you win in a game in which 96 percent of players die before their tenth anniversaries? Can you compete in this game? The time to decide is now. Not everyone is meant to be a business owner, but if you know this game is for you, why not play to win? Why not train like Michael Jordan and be an expert. I mean, what is at stake if you fail? What is at stake if you do not win the game? I know these are tough questions, but the business owner who fails to ask the tough questions fails to stay in the game.

During this journey, you need to involve your team with the questions and activities. If you do not have a team yet, ask your family, friends, or even clients to help. In business, as in life, it is no fun if you do it alone. You need to form a winning team.

I have provided my contact information below to help you along on the journey. I would like you to connect and message me on LinkedIn, and for doing that, I will make you an excellent offer. I will give you a gift that will really tie in with what you are learning. The gift will be a surprise until you message me on LinkedIn; everyone likes a surprise. If you are not on LinkedIn, take a moment and sign up. This is a business networking tool that as an entrepreneur you need to have.

Go ahead and connect and message me on LinkedIn now. Let's begin this journey together. Just ask me for the special offer in the subject line.

https://www.linkedin.com/in/dan-d-driscoll/

CHAPTER 1

Knowing Your Ideal Client

The Ideal Client: The Right Audience

> Profit in business comes from repeat customers,
> customers that boast about your project or service,
> and that bring friends with them.
>
> —W. Edwards Deming

If you do not understand your audience, you can easily get caught up in the rat wheel of business. According to Prato's 80-20 rule, 20 percent of your customers will make up 80 percent of your revenue and, more important, 80 percent of your profit. You can easily be caught up reacting all day to the normal excitement of your business and fail to reward customers proportionately to their value to your organization. When we treat all our clients the same, we miss out on the fact that only 20 percent of our clients are likely to be truly profitable customers. Understanding that these top-tier clients will make or break a business is essential when you are scaling and running the enterprise.

For instance, my girlfriend is a chiropractor. She loves what she does and treats every patient equally. She shows up to work purely to serve the clients. I totally respect her level of caring for her clients, and that is a key reason why she has been so successful in her field. However, if she is going to spend money marketing, do you think she should target clients who have a chance to bring in fifty times as much revenue per patient? Should she pan for gold or mine for silver? I mean, she could still treat everyone the same, but why would you want to attract an unprofitable client to your business? Many chiropractors fail because they love what they do but don't understand that profit is the only way they can sustain their businesses, and profit comes from your ideal clients, not your average clients.

So the first question to consider is, Who is the most profitable client for your business? The answer is different for each business. When I do consulting work, I ask five questions to find out who the business's most profitable clients are. I also show you how I used these to uncover the most profitable clients for my girlfriend's chiropractic business.

I know some of you do not yet have a business. If this is the case, apply these questions to where you work now. Or better yet, to the industry that you would like to start a business in. I also like to apply these questions to my competitors to figure out how they may have developed advantages over my business. Many successful businesses cannot really identify the reason for their success. By asking these questions, you will discover either why you are currently successful or the road map to finding your ideal clients. Remember, attracting ideal clients is the key to scaling your business and making a profitable enterprise that can sustain itself.

Questions to Ask to Find Your Ideal Client

1. Who spends the most per transaction?
2. Who buys with the highest frequency?
3. Who gets the most value from your product/service?
4. Who loves you?
5. Who refers the most clients to you?

When we started asking these questions with my girlfriend's business, we quickly discovered that her most profitable clients were not who she thought they were. Her best clients were not the clients who had chronic pain and came in all the time. Those clients were her most profitable individual billers, but they did not have the biggest impact on her practice. The clients who had the biggest impact were the ones who loved her and her mission and referred a lot of other people to her. When we looked at the clients who frequently referred other people to her, we realized they were either medical doctors or massage therapists. Love was only one component; the platform they used to spread the love was another.

Asking these simple questions, we discovered a way to scale her business quickly. When we did the math, we realized that two of her patients had referred over 50 percent of her new clients for the prior year to her. If she could effectively sign on four new patients identical to her two ideal clients, she could triple her number of new clients. Do you think it would be effective to market to perspective ideal clients more aggressively than you do to non ideal clients? I know the answer is yes, but many businesses forget this lesson and get slaughtered when they try to grow. They end up wasting marketing dollars on short-term, unprofitable clients. These business owners market to everyone the same. They fail to address the most profitable segment and ideal clients specifically with their marketing.

Many business owners make the mistake of marketing where the conversions are high in the short term but the yield to the business in the long term is nonexistent. Think about it. Have you ever received a coupon in the mail for something, gone to the business just because you got the coupon, and never made another purchase from that vendor? That business very likely lost money on you. Don't make this mistake with your marketing. Cater your marketing to the ideal client, who will provide long-term value. Take a minute now and find out who your ideal client is. You may even realize that you don't need to spend any additional dollars marketing to generate more business. You may just need to make sure your marketing and promotion are directed to the clients who can really move the needle for your organization, the whales.

The Client's Problem

> Don't find customers for your products, find products
> for your customers.
>
> —Seth Godin

The next question to answer is, What problems do your clients have? What problems are your clients solving when they hire your firm? In so many cases, the answer is not what you think it is. In my girlfriend's case, you would assume her patients were coming to her just to get out of pain. Although this is a major reason to see a doctor, there are many doctors who can heal pain. Why do clients choose one over another? When we started looking at this with her practice, we realized that her patients sought her out because other chiropractors lacked her personality and ability to truly listen and care.

My girlfriend listened and was able to discover the real problems they were having, the problems they would be willing to invest in fixing in the long term. For example, one of her clients came in for back pain, but the real problem he had was with headaches. He'd had these headaches for years. She diagnosed the headaches as an issue with his alignment and fixed both them and his back pain. The client was willing to come in monthly to continue to be rid of the headaches, but not for the back pain. For the back pain, he was very willing to ice it, hope it went away, and only see a chiropractor in extreme cases. But for headache relief, he is a raving fan.

Before I went to my girlfriend's business, I had been to multiple chiropractors. They were more interested in my wallet than my symptoms. I was never able to get on a consistent treatment plan because I just did not feel I could trust them. My girlfriend, however, took a lot of time to really assess my condition before treating me. She gave me options about my care and showed me that she cared much more about me than in making money from me. She really cared about my health in the long term, not just my short-term pain. My health was something I valued more than solving a simple backache. This was the solution she provided for me, and it was a solution that I truly valued. It caused me to continue my checkups and refer her tons of business.

Think about your business for a second. What is the obvious problem you solve for your clients? What might be another problem you solve that is the real reason your clients come to you and will continue to come to you? What frustrates your competition's clients about their services?

Try to look at this question from a lot of angles. This is your secret ingredient; it's important that you never remove it from your recipe as you expand. Most businesses run into issues when they stop doing something that works in exchange for some crazy tip they picked up from a guru of the week. Know what got you where you are today. It was a lot more than hard work. In my experience, it is normally only one or a few small things. We dive deeper dive into your offer in the next chapter. There you'll also learn how to communicate your correctly to your ideal clients. This is gold. This one lesson changed my view of marketing entirely.

Finding out what problem you solve is so important I want to show you another example to make sure you see it from more than just one viewpoint. As we do these exercises, think about your business, and start to come up with how your business can identify what problem you really solve for your ideal client. When I hired my swimming pool contractor, I was looking to build a crazy pool. Something that would satisfy my need to have a giant pool that everyone could come over and play volleyball in or swim laps in. Needless to say, I built a twenty-five-yard pool that could hold a few hundred people. But when I hired the contractor to build the pool, what was I looking for? What problem did I need to solve? Was it just to get the pool built, or was I building the pool for another reason? I did not really put this together until I got the bill and realized how much it all cost. I was putting the swimming pool in to impress all my family and friends. The pool was not about a way for me to cool off after a hard day's work. The pool had become a status symbol for me. The pool had turned into the emperor's gold crown. The pool was no longer a pool; it was going to be aligned with my identity. So the reason I was building the pool was to solve the problem of getting my house to be impressive, which would allow me to feel accomplished. I know this sounds sad, but this is often what many of your most profitable customers are looking for. They want to add to or reinforce their identities as being successful by purchasing your solution. In many cases, they will also want to brag to all their friends about their new purchases.

So I called the best pool companies in the area. All were ones I had either used to build or remodel a pool at a previous home or were referrals from trusted sources. When I got my three quotes, I realized that two contractors' bids were identical, and one was different. The different one treated me in a way that was nothing like how the other two treated me. The first two I called were very accommodating and able to meet me after work. The different one did not even return my call until I called the person who referred the contractor to me and complained about the business's nonresponse. A few days later, the contractor called.

The contractor refused to meet me after I got out of work. The contractor stated that he would not be able to answer my calls after work once he took the job, so if I could not take time out of the day to meet him, this arrangement would not work, and I should use another vendor. I found this interesting to say the least, so I treated it like a doctor's appointment and took a few hours out of my day to meet him. When we met at my house, his wife was with him; she was the pool designer. You could tell she was not a salesperson, but you knew she had good taste. She asked me many questions and got me to imagine the pool I wanted. But this pool was her vision, not mine. She knew that what I wanted I could not create. She knew I wanted an impressive pool, and I did not yet know what that looked like. But she sure knew what it looked like. She was able to get me to visualize her pool design in my backyard.

After we had the pool design, the owner simply stated that his goal as a pool builder was to stay small. He wanted to build only a few pools each month. He told me he turned down work from anyone that he did not know or anyone who cared about his price. Needless to say, he was the most expensive. Either way, I was buying the pool before I even knew the price. Long story short, I got the pool built and have referred a lot of work to him as well. This pool builder was able to align my future identity with his brand. He was able to solve the obvious problem as well as the real problem I had. Think again about your business. What are the real problems you solve for your clients? What problems do your clients have that they might not know about? How could you solve that problem? Just a hint, most clients are always looking for a way to be more significant. A way to brag to their friends. How could your product be something that they could brag about to their friends or colleagues? Do you need to add a premium product?

Now that you are starting to get a better picture of your ideal clients, it's time to get clear on their preferences. For example, when we looked at my girlfriend's chiropractic business, we realized that her ideal clients where massage therapists and nurse practitioners since they had a tremendous ability to refer her work. These were the patients who would provide the greatest long-term benefits to her practice. So what are the preferences of massage therapists? I know you may be wondering why I'm going over these examples, but trust me, this will help you get your wheels thinking about your ideal clients. Everything I'm going to do in this book has a propose, and my main goal was to eliminate the fluff. I want to give you a book with the meat you need to quickly make a measurable difference in your business. Stay with me. Massage therapists are health conscious, believe in alternative medicines/therapies, and tend to have a deep passion for their patients. You will probably not become a massage therapist if you do not believe in the work and want to help people.

Understanding your ideal clients will really help when we get to the next section, where we talk about your offer. Also understanding what happens right before a client comes into your business is key. For example, the reason massage therapists are great referrals is they tend to be the first line of defense for many people seeking pain treatment. When potential clients are in pain, they are often at a massage therapist and, in most cases, open to finding solutions to get out of pain.

The clearer you can get on your ideal clients, the less time and money you will have to invest in marketing. From all my years in consulting businesses, marketing is one of the least favorite conversations most business owners like to have. In the next chapter, you will learn how to save money on your marketing. You will really like the next section. And trust me, this offer is not the one you are thinking about.

But before we get to the next section, let's look at the pool builder and his ideal clients. Who were the ideal clients of the pool builder? It was someone who wanted to be seen, someone who believed in the best, and someone who cared deeply about appearances. Let's look at what kind of possessions this ideal client for the pool builder was likely to have. They would have a car that cost over $100,000, a house that was ten times the price of the average home in the neighborhood, and would very likely be a member of a fancy club or organization. These are just some of the points, but are you starting to get an idea why we obtain this information? It would be nice to know where to find these ideal clients, right? And more important, how to market to them.

Are you getting clearer on your ideal clients? Great! That is the point. As we get into the next chapter, this will make a lot more sense.

Activity

Let's apply this knowledge and turn this information into cash for your business.

1. Who are your ideal clients? Get descriptive: Describe them, make them into a buyer persona, someone you could talk to. Give your ideal clients names. Trust me, it will really help cut down on your advertising spending if you speak to your clients directly in your promotion.
2. What are the preferences of your ideal clients?
3. What are some of the things your ideal clients might own?
4. What are some of the things your ideal clients want now and in the next five and ten years?
5. What do your ideal clients really desire in life?
6. What are your ideal clients fearful of?
7. How could you protect your ideal clients?

Now that you have completed these questions, let's move on to the next chapter and learn about our ideal offers. It is beneficial to read both these chapters together, so let's get to it.

CHAPTER 2

Having the Right Offer

When you're just like everybody else, you've nothing to offer other than your conformity.

—Wayne Dyer

In all my years studying businesses and the three years that I was fortunate enough to sell Yellow Page advertising after college, I have yet to see a business owner blame his or her offer for the reason advertising failed. In my experience, the business owner's perspective was always that the advertising did not work, and not the offer specifically. I can tell you all advertising works, but most offers are horrible. I had clients tell me their Yellow Page ad was blowing up their businesses, and others in the same section of the phone book get no response and call me a scam. How could that be? I mean, could it really be possible that the offer matters? To give you an example. I sold a menu product to a Chinese restaurant. This menu product allowed the client to put the restaurant's entire menu in the phone book. When I met this owner, I asked the same questions that I asked every client I worked with: "What is your offer? Why would I choose your business over a competitor's?" This owner said to put a coupon in for buy one get one free. This is a pretty good coupon, and I'm sure you would expect it to yield some pretty good response, right? But here is what happened. I had another Chinese restaurant that also wanted to put a menu in the phone book, but this Chinese restaurant had a really good offer, not a coupon. By the way, a real offer is generally not a discount. But before I talk about it, I want to explain another offer to you.

I know you either have or know someone who has an iPhone. Apple has never used a coupon, but they have a really good offer. What is Apple's offer? If you are like me and use an iPhone, you understand that Apple's offer is the company, the brand, and the identity that Apple transfers to its users. Apple is a lot more than an offer; it is a movement. Now that you are starting to see where I'm coming from, let's return to the Chinese restaurant that had the competing menu. Their offer was killer, and it had no coupon. Their offer was simply when they opened, their background, and one bragging point. It looked like this: "St. Pete's Oldest Authentic Chinese Restaurant Family, owned since 1923, and home to the award-winning must-try Chowfung eggroll." Under the offer were testimonials about how you must try this eggroll.

Now let's examine this offer, so you can take the meat of this and add it to your offer. I had a client offering to give away his entire store that failed, and this client in the same section, only a few pages away, doubled the profitably of the restaurant. Why did this occur? The answer for me is simple, and this will be a game changer for your business once you apply it. The first business just looks like any other cheap Chinese restaurant. I'm going to enter the restaurant looking for a deal, and I will likely not return unless I can get the same deal or a better one. The issue with this offer is it violates the first part of the book. Who is your ideal client? This offer targets a price shopper and is using a system that will violate the next chapter by charging a price that will not allow, in this case, the restaurant to stay in business.

To put this in context, the average restaurant owner makes a profit of 10 percent of sales. Giving away 50 percent of the product is a loss leader. I know many restaurants have grand ideas of using discounting strategies, but they will only work if they are targeted. Meaning does your ideal client clip a coupon? I mean if your ideal client is super tight and cuts coupons, then great, do it. If you had a high-end restaurant, a better strategy could be to target high-end homes of couples who do not cook and love to drink wine. You could send them an invitation to a special dinner. You could say they were selected because they live in the prestigious neighborhood of X and have impeccable taste in wine. You could them tell them to reserve the seat early because there are only fifty tables at this high-end exclusive restaurant, and many of their neighbors have already reserved theirs. The entire family would receive a complementary dinner that includes X, Y, and Z. The meal alone would make them want to come. The restaurant would then talk about their awards and the difference that sets them apart from their competition, along with the wine list they offer. The offer of the restaurant might read,

> New York City's only true five-star restaurant. Michelin award winner Chef Mario Estefante prepares the best Latin fusion food in the city. And our wine host will give you the best dining experience you have ever had. Our wine host Amy Samarco, a winemaker for twenty-five years, will match your wine palette with our incredible cuisine to give you a dining experience that will have you raving to all your friends.

Now let's see why this offer is a game changer. The first thing the offer does is set the business apart from the competition. Now, remember I said you would not need to buy any advertising. I was telling the truth. Most businesses can just uncover their offers (why they are different than their competition), communicate them with their staff, and see business go up. I have seen internal communication of the offer alone produce more than 50 percent increases in profits. Simply getting your team to understand why you are in business and why someone would buy from you adds results. If your team just thinks you are another crappy Chinese restaurant, do you think they will sell as passionately to your clients? But if your team knows you have the best must-try eggrolls in the city, do you think they will recommend them to every patron of your restaurant? These little items really add up. The biggest thing you can do for your business is to have a good offer, make sure your team believes in your offer, and make sure the team understands how to communicate that offer. Remember, the best offers are not a coupon. They are the mission and identity of the company properly communicated through your team and through marketing to your clients. When your entire team knows your offer, it makes all your employees effectively salespeople for your organization.

For instance, when you tell me your offer, I should be able to understand your business and know if I should consider your enterprise. Your team should be proud to communicate this offer to your clients and their friends and families. Your offer should answer these questions:

Why would a client hire your business over a competitor?

What is your business really about?

The next thing the successful offer does is to take risk off the table. When you are dealing with food, this is pretty easy to do. When the offer says "award-winning," risk is taken off the table. If you have a software solution, you could do a free trial. If you sell food in the mall, you could give samples as people walk by. When you first start the process, acquiring a client's trust is low. The lower the trust, the lower the perceived risk needs to be to start the purchase cycle. Does this make sense? How can you make it easier for your client to try your service/product? How can you remove some of the risk? A thirty-day refund? A free sample? A testimonial from a super-happy user?

And remember online reviews are one of the best ways to take risk off the table for your clients. Have you ever made a purchase based solely on the reviews? Have you decided not to purchase something because it had no reviews or had bad ones? If you can't offer a special deal to get started, make sure you have a lot of good reviews to help offset the risk the client is taking to start the purchase. I have done business and I'm sure you have as well with a company simply because they have a ton of reviews online. **Potential clients who see your five-star Google status will often act like they are a referral from Google**. How cool would it be to have Google referring your work? Clients often feel they can trust and do business with you simply because of the reviews you have.

The last piece that both offers have is a way to create urgency to act. The first ad, since it is in the phone book's menu section, targets clients who are hungry, so urgency was handled by selecting the right spot to place the offer. The second offer, which is being mailed, needs urgency. The offer uses the urgency of having only fifty tables and that the event will sell out. **Without urgency, even the best offer will not work**. In my sales book, I talk about a ton of ways to increase urgency. I suggest you read it if you are looking for ways to create the right kind of urgency, the kind that will get your clients to actually make that purchase.

Three Things You Must Have in Your Ad

1. Differences between you and everyone else.
2. A way to remove/lessen the risk.
3. A way to create urgency.

> When you're just like everybody else, you've nothing to offer other than your conformity. (this is in here twice because it is that important). (Wayne Dyer)

Okay, let's look again at why the buy one get one free ad in the phone book failed. As humans, we learn most when we fail big. The reason you are reading this book is to save thousands of dollars by not paying the dumb tax. Learning from someone else's mistakes and feeling the emotional pain as if you made those mistakes may prevent you from making them. Our bodies remember our mistakes, but they can also remember someone else's if we feel them as ours. I would like you to try to feel that these are mistakes you made so you do not have to pay to learn these lessons; I want to use this book as a shield. Every mistake I talk about could ruin your business. In a small company, one dumb move could mean lights out, so let's play full out and safeguard your business.

One of the biggest mistakes is wasting money marketing to someone who is not your ideal client. The Chinese restaurant failed and went down swinging without a bat. Even if it got a hundred new clients from the ad, they would have lost money. Its marketing was targeting price shoppers, and it was an offer that was not profitable; it was a loss leader. In the next section, I talk about how to make your offer profitable and how the client purchase cycle works. I show you how to increase your lifetime value of your clients.

But before we go further, I want to talk about using testimonials in your offer. Testimonials allow your client to imagine what it feels like to own your product or use your service. Testimonials can also be used to answer your prospects' unspoken objections. Let's say you are selling a business-training solution that may solve a very complicated accounting issue the prospect is experiencing. The prospect may not be willing to admit he or she is not the best with technology for fear of looking weak in front of you. The testimonial could show an unsophisticated client talking about how he or she was scared to take on the project and how easy the training made the implementation of the solution. Testimonials turn your offer into reality in the prospect's mind. A good testimonial can easily close the sale.

I also like to use testimonials to remind repeat clients of the value that they could be getting from the solution. For example, if you sold a gym membership, how powerful would it be to show your members who are not using the membership a success story every month? This story would show them the value of your service, so they would focus more on the results they could have rather than the money they are paying for the unused gym membership. But it could also show them how much more value they could get by following up their workouts with personal training. Are you starting to see how important the offer is? How the offer is much more than a discount. Optimized ads are really worthless without the right offer and a good reason for the customer to buy.

When I'm working with a business, one of the first things I want to do is get the offer right. I always imagine that when I'm doing consulting that I need to provide value right away, or I might not get invited back. I know the right offer will add serious bottom line revenue to the enterprise. Remember, offers are not just about discounts. A good an effective offer shows why your business is different than everyone else's. Your offer should be a reason that someone chooses your business over the competition. Last, remember no one offer will satisfy every client. Your offer should showcase who should use your business and who should not. Think about a high-end restaurant. Do you think it should have the same offer as a side-of-the-road snack shack? Simply put, your offer should be directed to who should come to your business and who should go elsewhere. An offer needs to speak directly to your ideal clients. It needs to make them feel like they are in the right spot. Sometimes when I write an offer I even put in the offer who should not take advantage of our services. Sometimes I get more sales from talking about whom I do not want than whom I wish to attract. For instance, when someone reads all the things they despise and you have listed that these people should not come to your business, it can have a very strong magnetic pull in attracting the clients you want to your organization. I always remember the quote, "A jack of all trades and a master of none." You want to look like a master with your offer. You want to speak directly to your ideal clients.

Purchase Cycle

So now that I have shed some light on offers, it's time to talk about how to link your offer to bottom-line profitability for your business. If you understand your purchase cycle—or more important, client touch points—you can start to find all the necessary points you need to have an offer. Every time you interact with a client is a chance to have an offer. The majority of your offers should be to (1) make sure your clients are using your service, (2) remind them of the benefits of your product or service, and (3) talk with them about what is coming next, your innovations.

Think for a second. How does Amazon communicate its offers to its clients? They mostly use the third method. They are always talking about what new and exciting things are coming. They use this method as a strong hook to keep you using and renewing your Amazon Prime membership. Amazon wants you to feel that they are the only company to use because they are so far ahead of their competition. I mean, what competition? And their futuristic, innovative pipeline is bursting at the seams with cool new products you will want to use. Amazon has experienced the benefits of keeping almost everyone who has tried it by following this model.

Amazon knows that when they come up with offers, they need to focus on wowing their existing client base. Think about how a wowed client base could help your business. Or better yet, if they could not help but brag to all their friends about how you made their weekend amazing. Like, "Amazon was so awesome they got my shoes delivered the next day, so I had them for the party!" Or, "They got all my grocery shopping done for the party. I just came home, and everything was already unpacked and in my fridge. Thank you, Amazon."

When I look at a purchase cycle or a client contact schedule, I like to break down my client touches into (a) selling now and (b) selling in the future. All my touches are selling, but when I'm selling in the future, I'm working on the relationship and getting the client to see what is coming. I want the client to see so much value coming that he or she would never even think of leaving my solution for a competitor. The biggest issue I see with the majority of companies' client contact schedules is that they fail to work on selling in the future. Their marketing is all dollar focused in the short term. I like to think of marketing as making a giant pb&j sandwich. The bread is the relationship, and the peanut butter and jelly is asking for dollars. You want to alternate the layers of the sandwich by having some client touches that are all about the relationship and some that are all about revenue. Many marketing departments spend the majority of their day trying to find new leads and often fail to put up fences around their existing clients, allowing them to escape to their competitors. (More about this in chapter 5.) For now, just remember to put a fence around your clients, or have some other way to prevent them from quickly leaving your business. For example, it makes no sense to spend the majority of your day hunting for prospects and have no plan to keep them around the business. Selling in the future is how you put up that fence.

Example of an Offer I'm Using.

My goal with this book is to keep it short. Some of the concepts that I go over you will want to research further. You may even want to have me work on them with your business. But for now, just make sure if you contact me that you are serious about making some changes in your business. Do not call me if you are just on the fence about improving your business. The clients I work with demand excellence from their businesses. Staying the same or making small inflation-type growth improvements is not acceptable for my clients. If you know you are serious and willing to make the changes necessary to take your organization to the next level, message me on LinkedIn, and I will be glad to schedule a quick fifteen-minute call to see if we are a good fit. On this call, 95 percent of businesses are normally screened out. It is not because their businesses are not good. It's just that they are not committed to changing the trajectories of their businesses, and my solution only works for clients who demand a change in their businesses. If we are going to work together, we are going to focus on two things: (1) a commitment toward excellence and (2) a strong desire to learn while taking action, not one without the other. My service is not cheap, but then hopefully neither are your dreams. I have never had a client tell me the value they experienced from our solution was worth less than the dollars they traded. If this is something you want to do, message me now. Don't hesitate. Successful people act, and they act quickly and often.

The message I'm sending with this is an example and a sales pitch. I do not want to sell everybody, just my ideal client base. But I wanted to show you an offer that I use to sell my services. It is very passive offer, and it forces clients to step up before they call. My ideal clients have made a mind-set shift from this business is okay to this business sucks and has to change now. They are saying in their head, *I have to improve this business.* This was something that I uncovered when I was at USFCR. We were getting more than a thousand leads per week and closing less than 8 percent. The reason behind the close rate was lack of desire from our leads. Our leads were too green in the purchase process to talk with our sales staff about a purchase on their first interactions. So what we did was add a few more selling-in-the-future touches to the lead before the salesperson called. These touches educated the prospect on our offer. More important, they got them in a position where they actually wanted to talk with the sales rep. It also let the clients know who should do business with us and who should not do business with us. When we did this, we spoke right to the ideal clients to make sure they were more engaged with us. When our sales reps called the prospects, they felt like they were at home, in the right spot.

Now we are going to look at how to get our offer out.

Methods to Get Your Offer Out

Again, the purpose of this book is to make you money, not spend your money. I focus on free ways to get your offer out. These ways are also the most underused and effective ways that I know to increase the bottom line of your business, and the majority cost nothing. If you add these tactics to your current marketing program, your conversion and bottom line will improve, and in many cases, without spending any money. So without further ado, let's rank the best ways to get your offer out.

First, remember to tweak your offer to match your ideals client and each customer's contact points.

The Best Ways to Make Money with Your Offer

1. Educate your team on your offer constantly.
2. Test your team to make sure they know your offer (mystery shopper).
3. E-mail your offer to your clients.
4. Get your offers plastered on your website and in your physical office.
5. Get your offer aligned with all your current marketing pieces.

Notice how I did not talk about social media? I think so much effort is wasted on spending money in a marketing department—energy wasted on design, buying ads, and tracking conversions—that we miss the fundamentals. Yes, you will need to buy advertising, but until you master these core five, in my opinion, it does not make sense to increase your ad spend. You could have a great ad that gets attention, but if it does not set your business apart from the competition, you will likely not get many sales or, more important, long-term clients from that ad. I have watched videos of cats playing with yarn online that have received over 10 million views. Do you think the cat owners are making money off those videos? The answer is hell yes. But if you are trying to design an ad to go viral, why not just take a shortcut and buy an ad on someone else's already successful viral video? Or better yet, do you really think you could even attract your ideal clients from a viral video? I mean most viral videos are not viewed with the intent of making a purchase. I think you know the answer. In most cases, people watching viral videos are not the whales or needle-moving buyers that you want to target. So why do you want a message to go viral? **Your goal with any marketing campaign is to generate revenue. Do not forget this rule: Likes are not dollars.** And as far as I can tell, likes have no real bottom-line value. They do help inflate a business owner's ego, but they offer little bottom-line value unless those likes are from your ideal clients.

What is your current offer?

Why would someone choose your business over your competition?

How do you plan to communicate and reinforce your offer and message to your entire team (all-hands meetings, posters, flyers, e-mails, contests, tests, and so on)?

How do you plan to communicate your offer to your current and potential clients? Remember, current clients are more important; they are the only way to build a lasting business.

Who should not choose your business?

Who is your ideal client?

CHAPTER 3

Having the Right Pricing Strategy

How many times have you been in a business and wondered, *How can they stay in business selling this stuff so cheap?* I mean, they have such a razor-thin margin just one hiccup could force them to lose money. Profit margins are important in a business, but that is not what I'm talking about in this chapter. I'm not talking about raising the price of your service. But if you need to raise the price, by all means raise it. I'm talking about the long-term pricing strategy of your solution. So you have a one-trick pony, or do you have a long-term purchase plan for your clients. A purchase plan that is set up to maximize the per client value to the enterprise. A really good purchase plan will further increase sustainability of the future stream of earnings, put more simply, the resale value of your organization. A good pricing strategy increases the likelihood that your business will be around for the next ten years as well.

Think about how Hilton Hotels, for example, maximizes their value per client. To get this point across, I'll walk you through Hilton's pricing strategy so you can learn from one of the best. The first thing they do is sign you up for a Hilton Honors membership. This membership allows you to achieve tiers based on how many nights you stay. For example, I'm a diamond member at Hilton. Many of my friends know I have this perk, and some even want to have me book their rooms so they can get an upgrade and free breakfast. But how does this strengthen the clients' pricing strategy? This membership makes users start to think of ways that they can get their forty stays at a Hilton property to maintain their memberships. Hilton Diamond members have their status part of their identities and it's required that they stay a minimum of 40 nights per year to keep the status. They plan in the beginning of the year how they will get their forty nights. I mean, you get special treatment, including better service and a few free stays every now and again. The program really does not cost Hilton much, but think about how much that loyalty is worth to Hilton. **If you can give your clients a strategic advantage to choose your business over the competition, you are winning.**

Just to put it into perspective, the Hilton Honors program is considered one of the best rewards programs in the world. But other than the rewards program, what else does Hilton do to maximize their per client value? Trust me, they do a lot of wise things, and many of these will get you to thinking how you can maximize your pricing strategy. To start, when you check in to a Hilton, do they offer you an upgrade for purchase? Do they have a bar they promote? Do they have in-room drinks and snacks for purchase? Do they sell food? Do they offer to book local vacation tours for you, which they get a commission on? Do they e-mail you offers right after your stay to rebook another at a discount? These are all things that most hotels do, but the question is what can you do increase your purchase cycle? It is proven that the hardest sale is the first sale. So many businesses struggle because they do not capitalize on the easier and more profitable second and subsequent sales by their customer base. What is your second sale to your clients?

You want to have products that allow your client to grow into your solutions over the long haul, so they can envision themselves with your firm for the next ten years. For example, when I was in the Philippines, a scooter ride was around $1US to get into town at tourist pricing. The ride likely provided very little profit to the scooter driver, but what was the scooter driver focused on? He was focused on what I was doing during my stay. He was able to book tours, arrange further transportation, and so on once he had me on his scooter. This scooter driver understood the value of escalating the sale and moving the customer across the purchase cycle. Think about how hard it would have been for the scooter driver to pitch me a tour if he walked up to me on the street. It was much easier for him to pitch me while having a conversation as he drove me to my destination. After the ride is done, and I have confidence and trust in my scooter driver, it is also easier for me to consider the second stage of the purchase.

> If you want to fail in business sell all your customers ONLY one time. (Dan Driscoll)

Getting your pricing strategy right is so important. Without the right pricing strategy, you will be forced to be just another hamster spinning tirelessly in the business owner's hamster wheel of life. The right pricing strategy allows a business to create loyalty and bottom-line profits for the business. The cost to acquire a new client is super-high, and the stress required to regenerate your entire client list every year is very hard to impossible depending on the size of your business. The entire cost to acquire a customer is often not even understood by most business owners either. **When I think about my sales team and how much time they waste hunting new business, it sickens me. We spend our best working hours thinking of ways to create clients out of thin air, while we often fail to collect the low-hanging fruit of our existing clients because we don't have the time**.

Whenever I see this problem in my organization, I know it reflects on how well I designed and obtained the buy-in from my team on a true purchase cycle. If we just tell our teams to upsell and renew more, it will likely not work in providing the exponential growth that you deserve. When you design a purchase cycle for your clients, you want to make it easy for everyone in the office to understand and use the system. You want your sales team to see the reason behind the purchase cycle and how the products are set up to keep a client for the long term. Show them how long-term clients make their sales positions easier each year since they effectively have to cold call less and less each year as their book of clients builds. For example, when I roll out a new sales endeavor, I always want to offer a spiff to get my top performers to go out and quickly get a few sales. Once the company sees momentum from the sales reps, it can be easier to get everyone else on board with the long-term plan pricing strategy. When I was at USFCR, we had extremely low penetration on our marketing solutions, which were essential second sales in our purchasing cycle. I realized that this was a problem, and we put together a discount upgrade program to give a benefit to the clients to upgrade during the initial sales process. By doing this, we made it easy to ask every client for a second sale before we concluded the first sale. This increased our profits by 25 percent.

> Your best bet to maximize the lifetime value of your clients is to get the second sale closed immediately.
> (Dan Driscoll)

Let's look at a purchase cycle for popular motivational speaker Tony Robbins (worth over $400 million). Tony uses a great system to move clients from the first purchase to the second and get them to keep coming back for years. For example, in his model, he is able to get clients to go to the same seminar for forty years in a row. Talk about someone with a long-term offer and vision for his clients. His first purchase with his clients is either to buy one of his books online or to watch his documentary, *I'm Not Your Guru,* on Netflix. Both are low-friction, easy-to-generate first experiences. Once they have entered this first step, he passively sells his events and audio programs. His goal is to get his clients to research an event online and either book the event if they are ready or buy a tape course he offers if they are not as soon as they finish the first purchase. They are then added to an e-mail drip campaign to move them along to future solutions. Once he gets them on either of those first purchases, he promotes additional tape programs and seminars that would fit their styles. He offers twelve tape programs and six seminar programs in total. Once you buy all of them, he asks you to buy them as gifts for your friends. During each of his events, he sells products he represents from vendors that he is partnered with and on which he makes money. These include accounting services and exercise equipment. He also sells coaching programs that offer biweekly meetings with a life coach. He offers a free coaching session to anyone who buys a tape program to start this second sale process. Tony also uses an offer of value first with his entire sales presentation.

Lastly Tony has a super-tier called a platinum partnership for which he charges $85,000 per year. This Platinum Partnership provides the denoting as being a top spender and also helps justify everyone else going to multiple seminars and paying thousands for an individual seat. He gets his clients to use contrast and compare the $5,000 ticket price for an individual event vs. how much cheaper it is than the Platinum Partnership. The best part of the Platinum Partnership is how the members pay $85,000 each year and get access to the same six seminars as many times as they want for free and with preferred seating. This makes the average buyer feel like going to a seminar multiple times is a good idea and very normal. Tony's Platinum Lion badge is offered after you have been a Platinum Partner for over five years. He uses these Platinum Lions as testimonials to the value of his services to current and future clients. Once you are a Platinum Lion, you are offered more partnership opportunities directly with Tony. Tony's entire business model centers around being able to keep his clients focused on his solutions for the long term. He does not settle for his clients going to just one seminar. He has a plan for a client to grow with him and stay with him for years. He also offers business consulting if you want to buy an even higher package. He always has something for his clients to think about buying in the future.

Imagine how powerful it would be if you could have your clients follow a purchase pattern like this. Simply put, the formula for massive success in business is,

1. Attract clients.
2. Delight clients in the short term while focusing your team on finding out what would delight them in the long term.
3. Show clients a path to buying additional products/services. Show them what a lifetime relationship looks like, and get them excited.
4. Have a system to create urgency around the renewal and upsell points in the contact system.
5. Have a plan to turn your clients into your free volunteer sales force in which they refer your business 24/7.

Now when we look at the formula to make an insanely profitable business, where do most businesses fail? These expensive mistakes or failure points are often caused by a business owner's fear of selling or looking desperate. I will start with urgency around contact points to help shed light on the situation. Urgency is often viewed as pressure, and many business owners do not like when they are pressured. So they often assume that creating urgency with their clients should be avoided unless they are desperate. Many times urgency only comes when you have a sales goal that you have to hit or a bill that really needs to be paid. Both of these reasons create what I call desperate urgency. The definition of "urgency" according to the Google Dictionary is, "an earnest and persistent quality; insistence." The word "persistent" is used. Urgency is not effective without persistence, and more important, slowly applied persistence. I have often found that missing urgency is often the reason many businesses fail to continue to grow profitably. Many businesses simply hope that their clients create their own urgency, which in my experience, rarely happens.

> If necessity is the mother of invention, urgency is the uncle of change. Without it, progress slows and then stops and then reverses. (Nell Scovell)

The logical question now is how do you create urgency without creating a high-pressure situation for your client? This question, when answered correctly, will change how you do business. Let's look at some companies that do this very well to help stimulate your mind to think how you can integrate more urgency into your business. Apple has a great way of creating urgency when it releases a new product. Instead of just sending an e-mail saying the new iPhone is out, what do they do? The start doing a trailer, like the movies do: "Coming soon." They start to build excitement in the user for the coming product. Their goal is to get the user to make the decision to buy the phone before it is available for sale; they want the client to decide to buy in advance. They deliver this urgency through many channels. They list it on their website, in TV ads, in-store marketing, and so on. Their goal is to create a buzz around the product, so you think about buying your next product before it is even produced.

Think about how few things we upgrade that are not marketed to us. I mean, when is the last time you decided to upgrade your hot water heater? You could get one that would save you a ton on your power bill, but if no one markets it to you, will you still buy one? We use our phones and hot water heaters every day, but I have never thought about replacing my hot water heater till it breaks. My phone, however, I'm constantly thinking about upgrading and replacing. The strategy is getting me to apply the pressure on myself since I'm being shown something that is not yet for sale. Apple has given me an environment where I can, with no pressure, think about buying the phone before I can buy it. For example, if I'm shown something that is for sale, I will in many cases defend myself from being sold. But if it's not yet for sale, I'm more open to selling to me myself. In short, excellent urgency is created by getting prospects to sell themselves on the sale way before it is time for them to make a decision. The prospect's decision to buy is normally decided before the sales rep asks for the order. So it's essential that you have a system in place to allow the client to sell themselves before you ask for the sale.

For an example of this, let's look at a furniture store since I know most of you are likely not iPhone users. Only about 40 percent of us have an iPhone, wink, wink. Furniture stores typically have sales reps who are paid on commission, and the average shopper tries as hard as possible to avoid a salesperson. So how do the furniture stores create urgency? The answer can be found in how they use their promotional materials. One strategy that they now use is to get you to do a lot of pre-shopping at home. They have online tools that allow you to build your ideal room by entering in your dimensions and moving pieces of furniture around. These stores are getting you to presell yourself and create your own urgency.

When this is done properly, stores get prospects to walk into a store to purchase, not to shop. Think about how people just get in line at Apple Stores to buy the new iPhone. I mean, they have not even seen the phone, but they have already sold themselves on the need to get one before they sell out. Many people even get to the point that they can't wait another minute to not have the phone and take off work to get in line.

When you think about your business and urgency, remember you can do simple things to increase urgency that do not revolve around the closing table. Often it is what you do before the sale that really makes a difference on creating urgency and making sure the deal closes. One last point, clients are much more likely to do favorable research on a product before they are pitched the solution. After the client is pitched, he or she often looks for ways to justify not buying. In many cases, the client is fault-searching. The reason for this is that after you pitch the client, he or she often becomes fearful of making a bad choice. That fear makes the client very reluctant to sell himself or herself on moving forward. Think of the last time you did a lot of research before you met a salesperson. Did you buy quickly? Now think of a time when you did no previous research, were pitched an expensive product, and did the research after the fact. Did you find you were searching more for reasons to buy or not to buy? Were you trying to verify that the sales rep was honest, or were you looking at articles and research that would push you over the edge? If you look for dirt, you will find it, and prospects who do research after a pitch tend to look for and find dirt, they are essentially double checking the sales rep. You want to educate your prospect as much as possible before the presentation and definitely before you ask for the order.

So how could you get your clients to better educate themselves before you ask them for the order? Could you e-mail them a brochure, have a video they could watch? Remember, the more information you can get your prospects before they are faced with the decision to buy your solution the better.

Urgency can also be created simply by reminding your clients of the services you offer. Showing clients some additional ways your new product can be used can also create urgency in many cases. Showing a testimonial to your clients can sometimes create urgency. The lesson is simple: The best way to create urgency is to consistently stay in front of your clients. To not just enter their minds when they have a need but to always be in your clients' minds.

How the Consumer Buys

In today's world, consumers rarely buy what they need. We all know this. Think about a few things that you need to do or replace in your house right now. When I do it, I can think of my ineffective dishwasher and some broken sprinklers. And I also need to clean my fridge. These are just a few, and I really had to think about them. But then I change the question and think about the things that I want.

I want a Kangen water filter, new Ford pickup, and a trip to Madrid. Now I know this may seem like a dumb question to ask, but which actions do you think I'm most likely to do first? Yes, the ones that are in front of me the most. The Kangen water filter salesperson is persistent, always messaging me and bringing more water for me to have. The rep knows that if they keep getting me to use the product, Kangen will stay on my mind, and I will likely buy. Their strategy is working. Four thousand dollars for a water filter seemed like a stretch, but now that he is just bringing by water and letting me decide, I'm starting to create my own pressure. I mean, I get a gallon every week, but I likely drink a gallon of water every day. So do I ration the water to make it the week or buy a filter? I mean, he is getting me to ask myself a purchasing question every week when he brings the water. He is giving me a reason to buy the solution and giving me value every time I see him. He is showing me what I'm missing out on by not having the water filter.

Ford, for example, has never stopped marketing to me since I bought my first truck almost twenty years ago. They are always mailing me stuff about new models and how to better enjoy the truck I purchased. They even offer to buy back my truck since they have so few models for sale on the lot. They always make it feel like now is the best time to buy a vehicle, and if I do not do it now, I will miss out on getting top dollar for my trade and a low price on a new truck (urgency). Vacations are another issue. In general, they are marketed nonstop through social media today. Social media has really transformed how we experience the vacation business. Whenever I'm online, I'm constantly reminded that life is too short, and I need to travel or have some fun. It can be a very powerful motivator to see testimonials from your friends about how much fun they are having on their travels. Social media makes everyone think about vacations a lot more since this can be a large chunk of its posts.

I hope you have started to come up with a few ways to get your offer out to your clients. Now let's look at the consequences if you do not get your offer out properly. For my dishwasher, the thing is horrible; it barely cleans anything. I think I need a water softener or something to handle my hard water. But nothing is ever in front of me to remind me to do it or, more importantly, get me excited about it. If one of my friends had just gotten a great dishwasher, that could be the juice that pushes me over the edge. But unless something happens to excite me, I will likely wait till the dishwasher breaks. The successful appliance companies know this and market things like smart faucets and smart fridges. They create demand by promoting a reason to replace an appliance before it breaks; they create excitement around a boring appliance, creating demand. This is really key to all parts of selling. It is simply making sure your clients are aware of all the services that you sell and will be selling into the future. This allows clients to ask themselves buying questions before they have a need for your solution.

Let's quickly recap. The first thing that must be done to set up an effective pricing strategy is to have a system where your clients can grow with you. This means having more than one product. You want to have steps, similar to how Tony Robbins starts with a book, then a tape set, then a seminar, then coaching, then his $85,000 per year Platinum Partnership. This path is what keeps your clients engaged and gives you a reason to communicate with them constantly, allowing you to continue to occupy space in your their minds. My dishwasher company failed because they did not communicate to me about the next product, like Apple did about my phone. My Apple iPhone never breaks, but think about how often I get a new phone. The dishwasher is ten years old and sucks. But every one or two years, I get a new phone. It's because Apple knows the purchase path for me over the next ten years. Apple knows that I will buy a new phone as soon as one comes out with irresistible features or my phone is over two years old.

The next thing we need to do is create urgency around each buying point in our pricing strategy. Not urgency as in high pressure but in consistent exposure of your brand. You always want to have a reason to stay dominate in your clients' minds. You want them to constantly ask, "Should I upgrade my solution?" You also want them to visually see themselves using your future product/service. The last phase is really what makes great companies, and that is turning your clients into your volunteer salesforce for your organization. This is the holy grail of business expansion. I will not dive deep into this yet, but I want to plant the seed that referrals make companies, and setting up a system to help make it easier for your clients to make referrals is essential. Think about how you can create urgency around your clients referring business to you. Many companies offer rewards, much like a commission based around turning their existing clients into volunteer sales reps. One company I work with, for instance, offers free service for life if you refer ten people to its solution.

Now the last and most important piece of the right pricing strategy is diversification. In investing, there is no free lunch except diversification. Owning a business is inherently risky, And the likelihood of failure is higher with time. Every time the economy shifts, there is a chance that something bad happens with your business. Some businesses might not get wiped out during a recession, but the stress business owners face is, in some cases, far worse than even being wiped out. Having the right pricing strategy should be, at its highest benefit, a way for you to protect yourself from the next recession. I often tell businesses I consult with that hope is not a good strategy to keep a business safe. We all know that on average, there is a recession every ten years. The reason so few businesses make it past a decade is that they are unable to weather a recession. And the reason they can't is that they did not plan for the recession. They just hoped that it would somehow not happen, or something else would put them out of business before the recession. So the real question is how do we get your business ready for the next recession? How do we make it so that no matter what happens in the economy, you know that you are safe? Safe in that no one can destroy your baby.

In order to develop a good protection strategy to safeguard your business, we focus on diversification.

Diversification can be built into a business by,

1. Locations of clients
2. Types of clients—commercial, residential, government
3. Payment collection—one-time fee collection for multiple years or recurring monthly payments with long-term contracts
4. Product service offerings, meaning offering things that the client will keep buying, like shaving blades
5. Industry diversification
6. Real estate investments

The first and most basic is the locations of clients you service. If you only do business in your town, and your town loses a major employer, you could go out of business. Expanding geographically is the first measure of protection. The next level of protection is with types of clients. If you have government clients, they may spend more money and be stable no matter what happens in the economy. Having a surplus of residential clients can often make a business very dependent on the economy. Homeowners can cut back on items very quickly, whereas commercial and government purchasers often can't cut back on services in bad times. For example, I may quit my professional cleaning service for my house, but I will not cancel my service for the office if the economy softens. In today's economic climate, commercial businesses and government offices have much more disposable income, which can provide a lot of cushion during bad times as well as lots of upside during good times. For instance, if you get an average contract with the federal government, it could easily double your organization's revenue.

If you want to learn more about federal contracting, I suggest reading my book *The Four Paths to Success as a Federal Contractor.*

The next system is how you collect payment. Some businesses do not have contracts and allow all their clients to pay for services as needed. This method, although the easiest, puts pressure on your business in rough economic times, when clients may want or even need special incentives to renew with your company; some may not renew. Having a contract and offering a discount for loyalty can be a great way to help prevent your business from having cash problems during a recession, for instance. In many cases, it is only hard to sign a three-year contract once every three years, but a contract that needs to be renewed every year can be difficult to renew during normal conditions and impossible to renew during a severe depression. Having monthly payments on top of a multiyear contract can be even more beneficial since it prevents clients from being unable to make a large up-front payment at contract renewal. Many clients also have no problem signing a long-term contract after they have used the service for a few months and see the benefit, especially if they are given a discount. Many clients even sign a long-term contract before they start if they have a window to cancel if they are not satisfied.

The next one is product service offerings. This is a great way to build protection for your business. The best system was Gillette. They sold the razor cheap and made money off the blades. They realized it prevented the client from switching to another razor and provided them with more consistent revenue. They were no longer worried every time a client went to the store to buy a new razor that they could lose out. Instead, the client was looking just for the blades that fit their razor. This one idea was worth billions for Gillette.

Next is industry diversification. So many businesses are stuck in one industry because that's what they know. And this is often the biggest reason that businesses fail. It has nothing to do with being eliminated from a recession as much as it has to do with being eliminated through obsolescence. As a business owner, you need to fall in love with your clients, not your product. In many cases, your clients' needs and preferences will shift every year. You need to be flexible to move with your clients. For instance, when I first started my career, I was selling Yellow Page advertising. As the industry started to change and customers wanted more digital products, the company changed to an advertising company. The company had to pivot to stay relevant. Always keep your eyes open to other industries, and listen and watch your clients. If clients are leaving your business and spending their dollars elsewhere, become a detective and find out why. You might want to provide a similar offer.

And the last one is real estate.

I think real estate can be a great vehicle to add diversification to your business plan. I have often found that taking business profits and investing them in a source that will produce retirement cash flow is very wise. This cash flow can also be used to help supplement your income in case a dip occurs in the economy. The first step can be buying rental properties or other assets that can provide income to you in your retirement years. Needing to get 100 percent of your retirement income from your business is, in my opinion, not a good retirement plan.

So to summarize, **having the right pricing strategy is a lot more than the sticker you put on your product. It's having a long-term plan to show the customer what it looks like to be with your organization for the next ten years. It's having a plan that helps to protect your business during the next recession.**

It's setting up a system to make it harder for your competition to take away your clients focus. Having a long-term contract in place really helps prevent your client from noticing your competition. Last, it's setting a system in place that will allow you to win the game of business, to generate more passive income than you need to sustain yourself. A plan that is robust with multiple flows of income to protect your business. In my experience, when you master your pricing strategy, you have mastered your business. When your pricing strategy is well set up, your clients are always thinking about what they will buy next. They will clearly understand what you and your company will have for them in the coming years. This plan will build repeat business, loyalty, and referral clients.

What is your long-term purchasing plan for your clients?

What is your initial offer to clients? Is it one that takes risk off the table?

How can you communicate your purchasing plan to clients so they never look at a competitor?

How can you get your clients to see themselves buying all your products and staying with you over the next ten years?

CHAPTER 4

Giving Your Employees a Long-Term Reason to Show Up for Work

To get started, here's a quick checklist for the key items to keep your employees and culture right.

- Provide a career path for your employees, longer the better.
- Establish MUST & SHOULD rules for your employees, and make sure they know and understand them.
- Know what levers employees need to operate to make the most impact on the business. Make sure employees know what those levers are.
- Make sure employees are moving the levers that make the most positive impact on the business.
- Make sure your employees are removing low-value roles as they progress in the organization. A $50 per hour employee might not want to continue to perform a $10 an hour task they did when they were first hired.
- Determine if employees are reacting to events or being proactive and planning their days around key outcomes of the organization.
- Determine if employees are familiar with a culture of: accountability, measurement, growth, passion, and involvement.

- Remove the need for side hustles, get your staff on plan to earn a living wage.
- Make certain employees understand the mission of the business.
- Show your employees they are valued and appreciated.
- Involve employees in planning, let them in on things.
- Let employees help to solve challenges, even if you know the answer.
- Set up controls, such as a dashboard, to trust but verify employees and give employees access to a real-time scorecard.
- Be willing, as the owner, to give up some control.
- Take advantage of the power of multiple minds to make decisions, its not all you.
- Anticipate the future, and make certain to have a deep bench. Ask each manager who are their top four prospects to replace them.

Research indicates that employees have three prime needs: Interesting work, recognition for doing a good job, and **being let in on things that are going on in the company**. (Zig Ziglar)

If you want to own a real business, which I know you do or you would not have made it this far, the first thing you need are motivated employees. And not just motivated employees in the short term but motivated, engaged, and fully committed employees in the long term. The goal of a successful business owner is to have the daily operations of the enterprise be the life mission of the company's employees. Accomplishing this does not happen automatically. So many businesses have a great recruiting system but no viable plan in place to keep employees for the long term. In today's working world, employee disengagement is prevalent. Employees are often disengaged primarily due to lack of financial stability, meaning that many of your employees will partake in side hustles to pay for many of their daily survival needs. This problem is only going to continue to compound and worsen as technology makes it easier for employees to work remotely. This new environment creates many freelance positions that offer both full-time and part-time venues to compete for your employees' attention. For example, I had an employee who fixed iPhone screens part time. When this employee had a ton of screens to fix, he often called out of work sick. He chose to make $400 per day fixing screens over the after-tax $94.43 per day he could make with me.

As this trend of remote freelance work continues to grow and evolve, the workforce will need to be treated more and more like volunteers. Or simply put, we need to show our employees gratitude for the hard work they do and provide them with interesting and meaningful work. This was an idea that Peter Drucker started talking about years ago in his management writings. I believe that the cornerstone of the concept he was talking about fifty years ago has proven truer as technology has improved. In the past, employees often gave their bodies but not their hearts and souls to their employers unless it was something they believed in. Now it appears they will not even give their bodies if the mission is not aligned with their long-term goals. This shift has been fueled by options. For example, if you are working for less than $15 an hour, it is possible that you could drive for Lyft or Uber, quit your job, and not miss a paycheck. Twenty years ago, the workforce was terrified of losing their jobs. Now it is seen as a wise move to leave the grind and move into freelance work or entrepreneurship.

It is fairly clear that the internet and the options it has provided have changed the workforce quite a bit. There is a silver lining in this all. The best part about the internet is how it has allowed your standard employees to train and develop themselves. For example, you can hire an employee and have that employee become so passionate about his or her role and self-educate during nonworking hours. The employee will also take home work and stay connected after hours.

So how do you get your employees to go above and beyond? The first thing is to make sure that employees can see themselves in the organization in the future. And the second thing is to make sure they can see a steady growth in both rank and pay over that period. Once you have a handle on those two, we need to make sure we align the role with the employee. This can often be performed simply by making sure the employees are in on key business decisions. Employees need to have some control to dictate how they perform their jobs and have some form of financial incentive linked to that performance. Getting your employees focused on the overall outcome of their roles instead of on daily tasks they need to preform is the start of making this shift in your organization.

Quote from CNBC about millennials

Almost 90 percent of millennials surveyed in a new study said that they would choose to stay in a job for the next 10 years if they knew they'd get:

- *Annual raises*
- *And upward career mobility*

Most millennials are planning to stay in their jobs for at least six years, and 77 percent would be willing to take a salary cut in exchange for long-term job security, according to a survey provided exclusively to CNBC by Qualtrics, a Provo, Utah-based survey software firm, and venture capital firm Accel Partners (a Qualtrics investor).

Next I want to talk about rules. So many employers have so many rules that their employees can't see themselves working long term in their company. When I was a child, my mother only had three rules that I had to follow (1.Be respectful 2. Don't be foolish with your money 3. Do something you enjoy with your life). She had a ton of things that I should do, but only three things that I had to do. I suggest you do the same with your employees. You can't discipline employees every time they make a mistake and expect them to enjoy their jobs.

Ask yourself,

What outcomes do you want for your employees?

What rules must your employees follow (try to limit to three)?

What rules should your employees follow?

Now that sounds simple, but what could mess all this up? The first thing is if you fail to pay your employees a living wage. If you are hire employees because they are cheap, you will almost always be very susceptible to them being disengaged. For example, if your employees have bills they can't afford to pay, it will be hard for them to focus their full attention on your position. If you have an employee who needs to borrow $200 to pay the power bill before lunch, how will that person work during the day? This employee has a problem that needs to be fixed before he or she can actually get to work. Making sure your team does not have money problems is a necessity to prevent side hustle and disengagement.

The solution I came up with was a career path. On day 1 of a job, I like to show an employee what a three-year career path with the organization looks like. Then, after ninety days, we meet again and look at an optimistic ten-year career path. I want to show them the salary and titles that they could achieve and get them to buy into what a long-term career path potentially looks like. You're probably thinking, *I'm a small company. I do not have these positions.* Have you really thought about what your company could look like if it grew 10 percent a year? Have you ever considered running your company without hiring an outside manager, only promoting from within?

A company often fails to think about future promotions that will be needed if the company grows. For example, if your business grows at 10 percent per year, it will double in size in 7.2 years. This is based on the rule of seventy-two. Divide seventy-two by the growth rate of your current business, and that will tell you how many years before your organization will double. Many businesses fail to envision their organizations doubling, so they fail to train their teams for leadership positions they will need in the future. They effectively prevent their businesses from growing to their true potentials. Many business owners stunt the growth of their enterprises because they do not take the time to build tomorrow's leaders today. Lastly promoting from within is often the best value for the culture but also the bottom line. Often when I promote an employee from within I get more talent than I would get from an outside hire, with no ramp up period, all for less money. Most employees are so grateful for the promotion they are a happy getting a small raise with the title. Versus an outside hire will often compare the salary of the position to the salary of the market since they are shopping employers.

> Remember your business can only grow if it has capacity to grow. If you always run at a 100% capacity your team will not be able to take on that new client you need to grow. You never want to close your client acquisition because you waited too long to make a key hire. (Dan Driscoll)

When you go over the long-term career path with your employees, it can really help them see how these new jobs will be created. Many employees view their current companies as stagnate or dying. As an owner, your main role is to get your employees to see that with their full engagement your company will continue to grow to new heights, and with this growth, you will need new managers. When I worked at Verizon, I did not have clear optics on how I would get a promotion, and that was a main driver in why I left to work for myself. If I had could have seen progress in the near term at Verizon, I likely would have stayed. The message that I was communicated was that I would be a salesman forever and should be happy with that. Needless to say, that made me get motivated to leave the organization. **Employees who are disengaged will usually not tell you they are disengaged. Such employees check out three to six months before they actually quit their positions. Checked-out employees are cancers to the organization and need to be removed.** Constantly asking questions and getting feedback from your team is essential to maintaining engagement.

There are many ways to keep your employees for the long term, but I want to talk about the two biggest ones. The second-biggest one has to do with appreciation. Almost every employee who is disengaged feels that he or she is not appreciated. Employees often feel that their bosses are insensitive and do not care about them. This lack of appreciation is often the main driver in why an employee leaves an organization. When I first started managing employees, I often said that "My staff is ungrateful for all that I have done for them." Now that I have wised up, I know that my employees' job is not to appreciate me;

it's my job to appreciate them. Whenever you think your employees are ungrateful, it is a sign that you are failing at your number 1 job, which is to appreciate an employee. An appreciated employee will often be engaged just from the appreciation—if it is sincere. I know this may sound odd, but the power of appreciation is that strong. The tricky part with appreciation is understanding that just saying someone is appreciated rarely makes an employee feel truly appreciated. To really appreciate employees, you have to let them make key decisions in how they structure their day and achieve the outcomes you have set with them. You have to trust their judgment. You have to allow them room to make mistakes. You have to have clear expectations of their roles and how to measure the effectiveness of those roles. For instance, you can't just tell Suzie, "Thanks for all you do," and expect it to have a long-term impact. An employee wants to hear specifics around why you are acknowledging him or her. Employees want to know they are significant parts of the organization, and this can't be accomplished in most cases by pats on the back alone. Appreciation, in my view, is built around contrast. To whom do you compare your employees? If you compare them to how you would do it, you are f*cked. Would you work for what you pay? Compare your employees to the total value they provide the organization, and it will be much easier to appreciate them.

To show you truly appreciate an employee, do so when a person makes a mistake. Employees are often yelled at when they make mistakes. In today's business world, where change is constant, it is impossible to succeed without innovation. Innovation requires someone not to be scared to fail and to take risks. In short, if you have a great employee, you need to always being thinking about ways you can really appreciate that person. You want your employees to know that you genuinely feel they are essential to the organization. The mind-set that every employee is replaceable was a management model that I had heard in the past. This model barely worked years ago, and today it is a failing proposition for sure. Your team wants to feel it is a key piece in your organization and making a difference to not just the business but the community that the business serves. Your employees will need to do what is right for your clients, not the bare minimums of their jobs. By appreciating your employees, they will care about the business and want to do the things required to service the clients.

I think for any relationship to be successful, there needs to be loving communication, appreciation, and understanding. (Miranda Kerr)

The most important factor in keeping long-term employees is engagement. I feel strongly in the power of multiple minds. Getting the team together can be a huge strategy to keep the team together. A work environment can be so well built that people will not want to leave the office. It can be assembled almost like a social club, much how Google has done with its culture. Berkshire Hathaway has also built a community with its investors and individually owned businesses. CEOs of Berkshire-owned companies will often turn down higher-paying jobs because they do not want to leave the Berkshire family. Having team meetings helps to further increase not only the team building but the significance of each member to voice concerns about the operation of the company. All employees have ideas, and creating an environment that allows them to share their ideas is essential in maintaining long-term employee engagement.

A sign of engagement is when employees go above and beyond to contribute their thoughts and ideas to improve the organization to upper management. (Dan Driscoll)

All-hands meetings, in my opinion, should be done often. Many successful companies have them monthly; some even do them weekly. These companies are forming a culture that is almost like a country club. The employees are really drawn to the social environment, and this helps to further separate your position from one at another company. If you think about volunteers and how much they enjoy volunteering and relate it to companies that give back a piece of their profits to social causes, you can see some reasons behind it. **Ninety-three percent of volunteers are engaged in their volunteering, while less than 40 percent of employees are engaged at work.** Having a mission that serves more than your bank account can really help give your employees a reason to work for you for the next ten years. Remember to keep engaged and productive employees for the long term, you have to treat them like volunteers.

You must appreciate them for showing up, tie what they are doing to the greater good, and give employees flexibility to control some aspects of how they contribute to the organization. Lastly having a mission bigger than the bottom line does not have to be expensive. Salesforce.com a 13 Billion dollar company that is considered very philanthropic donates 1% of the profits 1% of the equity and 1% of the employees time to charity. If you made this small commitment to your business how much goodwill would you have to get back to make it worth it? I mean salesforce.com turned this model into a 13 Billion dollar organization with employees that truly care.

Ask yourself these questions to learn about employee engagement in your company.

1. When is the last time you had an all-hands meeting?
2. Do you have a plan for each employee to know how to achieve his or her next promotion (what they need to do and the pay scale of that job)?
3. Is there a three-year plan for each employee?
4. Do you have a ten-year career path for each of your employees?
5. Does each team member make a living wage?
6. How do you appreciate your team nonverbally and verbally?
7. When is the last time you said your employees were ungrateful?
8. Do all your employees submit ideas for ways to improve the business?
9. How many cars in your parking lot have ride-share stickers on them, meaning they moonlight as Uber drivers?
10. Do you yell at your employees when they make mistakes?
11. Do you give employees the ability to have an impact on how they get their outcomes?

These are just a few ways that you can increase employee engagement. I have worked with both engaged and disengaged employees. I can tell you that disengaged employees are worthless. Engaged employees are excited to come to work, and they will also make you excited to come to work. **Remember, when you manage people, it's about them, not you. Your job as a leader is to meet the needs of your team first. Then your team's job is to meet the needs of the clients. It all revolves around the clients.**

Lastly when a team member is promoted, it means the person is great at doing his or her job. But the employee often lacks necessary leadership skills. The team member earned a promotion but was not prepared for all its aspects. Getting an employee trained to be promoted well before the promotion is given is essential to maintaining engagement and in developing a successful promote from within strategy. A new manager should never forget his or her main job is to meet the long-term needs of the team.

In conclusion, if you are succeeding at business, you are promoting from within. Your employees are always following a career path and constantly developing so they can replace their current boss well in advance of the position being open. Promoting from within is essential to have a rock star organization. To promote from within, you have to plant seeds far in advance. Little Suzie might need five years' experience before she can manage a team. You need to start training her now, so she is ready when the time comes. Also, when you hire a manager off the street, the person needs at least six months to be competent in the role. And this does not include how much you piss off the other employees who missed out on the promotion. Employees hate to see managers hired from outside. Trust me on this one. When I look at my team, I try to identify the best person to replace me and the best person to replace that person. Thinking about the future gives you a better ability to predict what is coming. And if you are going to grow your enterprise at 15 person per year, you will double in 4.5 years. Do you have the plan in place to train the leaders you need for tomorrow?

What does your career path look like for each employee for the next twenty-four months? What skills do they need to learn? Who do they need to become?

What do your current employees think about working for your company? Do they feel they can get promoted? Do they feel your company does good for your clients?

How can you identify who is the best fit for each future management position?

How can you start training your next manager?

How can you get your employees to feel they are in on key things?

How can you get your employees to feel loved and appreciated?

How can you get your company to be about more than just making money?

How can you increase the engagement of your current employees?

CHAPTER 5

Having a Good Plan to Keep Your Clients

Here are some quick bullet points for you to consider before you read this chapter.

- How do you align and prioritize your marketing department's resources/focus between new and existing clients based on the bottom-line impact of the segments?
- How do you set expectations for new clients?
- How do you reset expectations for existing clients?
- How can you deliver more than the client expects?
- How do you get the client to use the service/product more?
- How do you get the client to associate their identity with your solution?
- How can you get your client to brag to friends about your service?
- How can you make the product so good a client will never leave you?
- How can you remove the time it takes to renew your service?
- How can you make it easier to buy.
- How can you turn your clients into volunteer salespeople?
- How can you get different client types to protect your business during economic downturns?

- How do you get financing in place for your clients during rough times?
- How can you get feedback from clients to understand their desires and fears?
- What changes could affect this audience's ability to purchase?
- Why would this audience leave your competition for you?
- Why might your clients leave you?
- What do you do now that frustrates your clients?
- What does your competition do now that frustrates your clients?

Increasing customer retention by 5% boasts profits by 25%-90%. (*Harvard Business Review*)

The best way to keep your clients is to turn all your clients into volunteer sales people for your organization. *A volunteer sales person is a client that is so happy with your service they tell everyone they know to do business with you.* Apple has built a Trillion-dollar company by turning its clients into volunteer sales people, it works!! And no commission needs to be paid either. (Dan Driscoll; emphasis added)

The reason keeping your clients is the last section in the book is that without the first four things, you can't keep clients. Many business owners think that keeping a client is a once-a-year strategy performed around contract renewal. Or maybe it's even more a matter of luck than anything else. But keeping clients is the only way I know to sustainably grow a business. You can't churn and burn your clients and be successful in the long term. Now some business owners, including real estate agents, think that they can't get repeat business, but the truth is the average person moves every five years. And that person likely knows someone every week who is looking to buy or sell a house. Your existing clients are your volunteer sales force. Whether they buy another product from you is irrelevant. The satisfaction and loyalty of your clients compute the value of your organization. Keeping your current clients is more about continuing to occupy space in your clients' minds past the buying and renewing points. A good plan to keep your clients is built on the foundation of linking what you do to being the clients' go-to person. For example, your client should say, "You should use my real estate agent," or, "You should go to my chiropractor." Getting this kind of loyalty is the sticky factor that will lay the foundation for your business to scale.

A good plan for keeping your clients begins by putting up a fence to make it hard for your clients to wander off. This fence can be put up by setting up recurring billing or using long-term contracts. The fence alone is not super-effective because if someone really wants to leave, he or she can easily jump the fence or find a way out. Also, when clients want to leave, they will no longer be providing goodwill to your business. In many cases, they will no longer refer clients to you. Despite their lack of dependable effectiveness, fences are still essential as they help you keep your clients during a recession, when they may be forced to make cutbacks. The fence is a great idea used by many companies as the primary way to keep clients.

The more effective strategy is what I call the feeder. I like to think of my clients like livestock. The more livestock I have, the more money that my business can make. I believe that a business does not make money in the long term until it develops relationships with clients who repurchase and refer. These clients can be referred to as the livestock of the business. The longer you keep the livestock, the more valuable they are. For example, you can turn clients who have been around for twenty years into testimonials to show your current clients as examples of what it looks like to be with our company for twenty years.

Now that you have a good handle on how important it is to have a way to keep your clients by having both a fence and a feeder, the question is what is the best way to do this? In my experience, the best way to put up a fence is to have some form of contract or recurring billing system. Some companies, like Apple, are able to put up a fence with an additional service, creating a "sticky factor," like iCloud, the service links your desktop computer with your phone. This small service makes it hard to switch from an iPhone to another device because you would have to resync all the data. Other companies, like Microsoft, have a complicated product to understand, and once you learn how to use it, it is very hard to switch because of the time needed to learn a new service. Amazon has also managed to put to a fence up with its service by setting up one-click purchasing. This system, although simple, has been a huge driver in Amazon's growth. Clients do not want to waste time, and this saved login information got Amazon its start. Amazon was able to take their clients' trust in their book business and move into all their other offerings they have today. A simple fence can be the springboard to grow your business exponentially, just like Amazon did.

> 84% of buyers start the buying process through referrals. (*Harvard Business Review*)

The only true way I know to maximize your client relationships and thus your referrals is to put out a feeder. A feeder is simply a strategy that keeps your organization on the top of mind of all your clients. It prevents a situation such as when someone asks your client who his or her chiropractor is, and the client answers, "Ah, ah, I can't remember. But the office is located off Sixty-Second Avenue. I will have to check." You want to make sure that your clients are so grateful and happy with your service that they actively look to recruit their friends and families to join your organization. At its best, a feeder turns your clients into volunteer salespeople for your organization. The best way to think about a feeder is to set up a way to deliver more value than what your clients expect. Delivering your clients value above what they expect starts to activate the theory of reciprocity. Clients will want to do something to repay you for what you have done for them. The old saying, "If you want more give more," is so true with your clients. Often the best way to turn a regular client into a volunteer salesperson for your organization is through consistent overfeeding. This should not be a year's worth of food put out at one time but a constant drip of food. Enough to keep the client full and happy. So many businesses make the mistake of forgetting to keep in touch with past clients that they feel do not have the ability to purchase more. This is a huge mistake. Your business is built off the backs of your first clients. Charles Schwab said it best: "Never lose a client."

It's a good idea to think about tiers of clients when you establish your feeder. We then want to think about how we will feed each tier

THE FIVE THINGS YOU CAN'T F&CK UP IN YOUR BUSINESS

based on their value to the organization. When we talked earlier about my girlfriend's chiropractic business and how her ideal clients were massage therapists and nurse practitioners, the reason for this was both of these clients tended to refer her a lot of work. These were what she identified as her first-tier clients, those she would want to feed more often. Some of the ways she might feed these higher-tier clients include (1) offering to take them to sporting events, (2) hand-signed thoughtful birthday cards, (3) small gifts, (4) free care from time to time, (5) recognition on a board at the office for the number of patients they referred, (6) thank you cards each time they refer someone, and (7) special discounts to patients they refer. These are all ways to keep the relationship alive. You want to make sure that when you work with a tier 1 client that you keep them so full they would think of puking if they even just looked at one of your competitors. Remember, the clients that you most desire are often very desired by your competition, so overfeed them so your competitors can't show up on their radar. It's essential to keep your tier 1 clients focused on how they can refer all their contacts to your organization.

Tier 2 patients may be her most loyal clients who do not meet the highest referral potential. For these patients, my girlfriend may offer discounted service, personal thank yous, hand-signed birthday cards, and acknowledgment for referrals. Then for all the remaining patients, she would simply have a system to stay current in the clients' minds. These could be holiday cards, generic birthday cards, and e-mails about how to have better health. Even providing education and engagement on social media can effectively feed your clients. I like to think of social media as the most economical platform to keep current with your clients. If you friend all your clients on social media, you can always have a system to talk to them by posting. But the only way to maximize the platform is to feed your clients a constant drip of content. Staying relevant in today's world of distractions requires about sixteen touches a year. It used to only require about four. I feel that number is going to continue to increase as people look at social media now two hours and twenty-two minutes a day according to a 2019 study by Digital Information. My suggestion is to try to find a way to get the sixteen touches on all your clients using as many strategies as possible. Provide them with the feelings you want them to have about your business with each contact, and make sure they never forget your organization.

You want them to feel that you are their chiropractor or their accounting firm. Whatever business you are in, you want your clients to feel that they are important to your business. As Steve Wynn (owner of the famous Wynn Hotel and Casino) says, make your clients feel important, and they will give their loyalty. Sometimes even a phone call can be an effective way to contact a client.

Remember, when feeding clients, it is important that we separate feeding and sales/marketing, or at least make sure that the overwhelming message is food, not sales. Overselling is a problem in today's world, and it can push clients away, especially if it comes off as greedy or dishonest. Remember to sell like Apple. Brag about what is coming or show success stories, give information. Our main goal is to maintain the space in our clients' minds for whatever our business is.

To summarize, keeping your clients is not a once a year thing. Keeping a client is about keeping your product or service in your clients' minds. When this is done effectively, a shield will be erected that prevents competitors from stealing your clients. Your clients are like your livestock. The more livestock you can keep and the older your livestock get, the more profitable your business will be in the long term. Transactions are meaningless in computing the long-term value of your organization. The only things you really keep long term are your livestock, and their health is far more important than a series of one-time transactions. It's like the saying goes, "Do not kill the golden goose that lays the eggs." Your clients are the golden geese. You never want to let a small issue stop a future stream of earnings.

Last, you want to make sure to have a fence up to make it hard for them to switch during bad times. But the only real way to keep your clients long term is to feed them. Feeding clients should be based on the long-term plan for the livestock. You should group your clients into at least three tiers and feed them accordingly. A good system will result in about sixteen client touches per year, allowing your brand to always be at the top of your clients' minds. These touches include anytime clients come into the business and you or your team interacts with them. It is best to split these up as evenly as possible throughout the year. Clients have a lot going on, and taking a few months off from feeding your clients could easily cause them to stray.

How can you communicate what is coming to your existing clients?

How can you get your clients to see the total value in your solution?

How can you put up a fence to keep your clients?

How can you get your clients to see themselves with your organization for the next ten years?

What channels can you use to feed your clients?

CONCLUSION

The most important thing to remember in business is not to f*ck up on any of the five things we went over. Making a mistake on any of these items could prevent your business from reaching its potential. The first thing to think about is your ideal client. When we talked about an ideal client, we were not just talking about your favorite client. We were talking about the client who would move the needle for your business, the whales. Think about the client who if adding just one would change your year. These clients are often capable of referring other large clients or providing life-changing testimonials of your organization. **When you market, do not forget the importance of focusing your marketing on your ideal client.** So many businesses error on spending dollars to acquire conversions and clicks. The point of marketing is to acquire clients who can move the needle. Marketing, again, is not about clicks. It is about connecting your businesses with your ideal clients, who are the building blocks of a lasting organization. You may never turn down a client, but you do not want to waste money marketing to unprofitable ones.

The next essential point is to understand your businesses offer. Remember that your offer is not the price. It is the reason you are different than your competitors; it's your DNA. The biggest way to grow your business without any investment is to train your team on your offer. Your team should be able to quickly say why you are different from the competition and why prospective clients should choose you over the competition. Alignment and buy-in of your team on your offer will form the culture that your clients want. Think about how hard it would be for your team to deliver on your mission if they did not know it. Getting deep understanding of your company's offer and mission by every member in your company is essential to maximizing your business.

The third thing we went over was your pricing strategy. Your pricing strategy is the system that will get you out of the rat wheel of business ownership. Having the right pricing strategy allows you to set up the business to be winnable. A good pricing strategy gives clients a vision of things to purchase now and into the future. If your clients are constantly looking at the premium models you offer, for instance, they are not looking at the competition. In many cases, they are focusing exclusively on your organization for future purchases. Also, the correct pricing strategy will make it easy for your clients to start doing business with you.

The best pricing strategy will take the risk off the table for new clients to try your organization. Once they experience the value of your organization, it will be much easier for them to continue to buy more and more expensive packages. Remember, the first sales are the hardest, and the second sale is often the most profitable. Never let your clients run out of ways to continue to do business with your organization. Give your clients ways to start small and spend more as the trust in your organization grows over time.

The fourth thing you do not want to f*ck up is your strategy to keep your employees. Without a good plan to keep your employees, you will always have a job. When you have a system in place to make your employees truly feel valued and a part of your organization, you have a culture. **Culture is key to long-term business success**. You want each member of your team to care about the organization and show up for more than a paycheck. The most basic way to accomplish this is to have a long-term career path for every employee. This path allows employees to see themselves in an organization for the long term. The next essential step is to make sure your employees feel they are in on things. And it's important that employees feel heard and appreciated. Not every idea will be executed, but every idea shared is a sign that your employees care about your organization. You want to seek out your employees' inputs and ideas. The fact that they are thinking about the entire organization and doing more than their initial jobs are signs of good leadership. Remember, employees don't leave bad organizations; they leave bad leadership. Be the leader who appreciates and challenges your team. The leader that makes them want to step up and reach for more.

The fifth thing you can't f*ck up is the most important, but without the first four, keeping your clients is like a game of Russian roulette. Without a solid plan, your clients' continued business can seem more like hoping than knowing. Having a system in place to make sure your team knows why your company is unique, and communicating that message is essential to keeping your clients. When I work with a company and design a plan to keep clients over the long haul, the first thing I want to understand are the methods of communication with the clients. So often the marketing department focuses their communications exclusively on new business. This new business push seems to be rewarded by business owners since they remember when they first started their businesses and the value of having new business. As the business ages, it becomes much more important to adjust the focus of the marketing department based on the revenue of the organization. For example, if 90 percent of your revenue comes from repeat and renewal business, do you think it makes sense to have 90 percent of your marketing department focused on increasing the renewal percentage of your business? One of the questions I like to ask is, **"How big would your business be if you never lost a client?"** When we think about this, it is also easy to look further and ask, "Do we even need new clients? I mean, could we live on our client base and referrals if we maintained a high enough engagement with our clients?"

The main lesson from this book is to make sure you are running your business proactively and not letting your business run you. **Taking time out of the day to think about your business' future is essential if you want it to have a future**. Companies like Amazon are so successful because they are able to think seven to ten years in the future. They are able to keep their clients' focus and attention in the long term. Amazon clients are so excited about the future of Amazon, they are not looking at any competitors. You can't shop what might be coming. Amazon wows its clients so much in many cases they are unable to even notice a competitor. This may seem like an advanced concept, but Amazon's communication is designed to talk to its customer base, not new clients. Amazon knows the importance of maintaining the future focus of their customers.

Amazon also knows the benefits of its employees. Amazon has chosen to give stock options to its employees because it wants to have all its employees think like and be owners in the organization. Amazon makes sure all its employees have a long-term purpose in the organization and that they all see a path to becoming owners in Amazon. In many cases, the employees gain ownership their first day at the company, when they get their first shares in their 401k. I know you may be thinking you can't give out ownership, but can you give out bonuses based on performance? Can you tie employee bonuses to the bottom line of the business so your goals are aligned with their goals?

I want to leave you with this simple message. Life is what you make it; business success is not what you make of it.

> Business success is simply a measure of how well your organizations culture is able to actively engage your team in coming up with the solutions to meet the needs of your clients in the long term. (Dan Driscoll)

I wish you well in business and hope that one day we can meet. I would love to hear how this book has had an impact on your business. Again, my contact info on LinkedIn is https://www.linkedin.com/in/dan-d-driscoll.

Make today day 1 of building the business of your dreams. Take action and begin. Look forward to seeing you soon.

APPENDIX

The Successful Business Owners' Workbook

CHAPTER 1: KNOWING THE IDEAL CLIENT

Which client type purchases the most from you?

Which client buys the most frequently from you?

Which client refers the most?

Which client is the happiest with your service, really loves you?

After you have identified them, we want to calculate who is worth the most to the organization. Use rough numbers if you do not know, but clarity is power in these numbers

Average value of a client purchase =

Average times a client buys from you per year =

Average number of years a client stays with you =

How to Calculate Average Client Value

Multiply average purchase value times average purchases per year times how many years a client stays with you. This is a good number to have.

Average Value of Purchase	Average Number of Purchases per Year	Average Number of Years a Client Stays with You	Total Lifetime Value of Client

Now let's look at how many clients are referred by your ideal client. For example, if you have an ideal client who refers you ten clients per year, and each client has a lifetime value of $10,000 to your organization, that one client adds $100,000 per year in lifetime revenue to your organization.

Now that you are doing the math and finding out who your ideal clients are, let's find out more about them.

Who are your ideal clients? Describe them; create a buyer persona, which is simply a very good description of the buyer. Once you have that, name the persona. You want to be able to speak to this persona when you do your marketing.

Where does your ideal client shop?

Where does your ideal client live?

In what things is your ideal client interested?

What is your ideal client scared of?

How can you protect your ideal client?

How can you reward your ideal client for referring work to you?

How can you continue to wow your ideal client?

CHAPTER 2: HAVING THE RIGHT OFFER

What is your offer?

Why should someone choose your business over the competition?

Who should not choose your business?

How can you communicate your offer to your staff?

How can you test your offer with your staff to make sure they understand it?

How do you communicate your offer in the different client touch points?

CHAPTER 3: HAVING THE RIGHT PRICING STRATEGY

How do you reduce the risk for clients to start doing business with you?

What products would a client buy who stayed with you for ten years?

How do you keep your clients focused on your next solution and keep them from looking at the competition?

How do you align your pricing strategy to increase as a client's trust grows, meaning we start with a low-price solution and move to more expensive solutions in time?

How do you communicate to your clients at each of the points in the purchase cycle?

CHAPTER 4: GIVING YOUR EMPLOYEES A LONG-TERM REASON TO SHOW UP FOR WORK

What is the career path for each employee?

How do you get ideas and feedback from all your employees?

How do you show your employees they are significant parts of the business?

How do you show your appreciate to your team for their hard work?

How do you make your entire team feel like they are in on things at the business, that they know what is going on.

What are the desired outcomes for each of your employees?

What is the measurement system is used to determine if employees are hitting those outcomes?

What is the reward system to compensate employees as they hit their outcomes?

How can you give an employee flexibility to hit the outcomes and not be so task-focused?

CHAPTER 5: HAVING A GOOD PLAN TO KEEP YOUR CLIENTS

What is the fence that you put around your clients? Is it a long contract, high switching costs, integration into other aspects of their lives?

How do you feed your clients based on the tier they are in? How do you reward them for staying with you? How do you delight them? How do you give them more than they expect?

How do you turn your clients into volunteer salespeople for your organization?

How do you get your team to constantly understand the long-term needs, wants, desires, and fears of your clients so they can design the solutions your clients will need in the future?

www.ingramcontent.com/pod-product-compliance
Lightning Source LLC
Chambersburg PA
CBHW021502210526
45463CB00002B/853